St. Paul's Anglican Churchyard O - R

The Grave Whisperer

Angeline Gallant

Published by Angeline Gallant, 2022.

ST. PAUL'S ANGLICAN CHURCHYARD O - R

First edition. September 13, 2022.

ISBN: 979-8215663462

Written by Angeline Gallant.

Table of Contents

DENNIS O'REILEY[1]

Dennis was buried on April 18, 1809.
A church was built over his grave.

CHARLES OLIVER[2]

Charles was born in 1795.

He was 46 years old when he passed away in 1841. A church was built over his grave.

EDMUND JOHN OLIVER[3]

Edmund passed away in 1816.

A church was built over his grave.

JOHN OLIVER[4]

John passed away in 1813.

A church was built over his grave.

CATHERINE OLKOT[5]

Catherine was buried on March 23, 1807. A church was built over her grave.

ANDREW OLSON[6]

Andrew passed away in 1811.

A church was built over his grave.

WILLIAM OWEN[7]

William passed away in 1815.

A church was built over his grave.

JOHN PAGE[8]

John was a seaman when he was buried on April 22, 1795. A church was built over his grave.

JOHN PAINE[9]

John was buried on August 13, 1792. A church was built over his grave.

JOHN PARKER[10]

John was buried on August 5, 1804.

A church was built over his grave.

JOHN TURPIN PARKER[11]

John passed away in 1818.

A church was built over his grave.

ALDHAM PATRICK[12]

Aldham was born on October 29, 1799 in Kingston, Frontenac, Upper Canada, British Colonial America.

He was 13 years old when he passed away on April 20, 1813. A church was built over his grave.

JERMYN POYNTZ PATRICK[13]

JERMYN WAS BORN ON October 10, 1765 in Barking, Suffolk, England.

He was a church warden and the watch and clock maker of Kingston, Upper Canada.

Jermyn was 25 years old when the first parliament of Upper Canada assembled on September 19, 1791.

He was 44 years old when he passed away on June 21, 1810. A church was built over his grave.

SARAH (ALDHAM) PATRICK[14]

Sarah was born in England on March 29, 1765.

She was four years old when the Boston Tea Party took place in 1770.

Sarah was 25 years old when the first parliament of Upper Canada assembled on September 17, 1791.

She was 45 years old when her husband passed away in 1810.

Sarah was 48 years old when her only son, Aldham, passed away in 1813.

She was 78 years old when she passed away in June 1838.

A church was built over her grave.

SUZANNAH (BULL) PATRICK[15]

Suzannah was born in England.

She passed away on February 25, 1812. A church was built over her grave.

WILLIAM POYNTZ PATRICK[16]

William was born in England in 1733.

He was three years old when his mother passed away in 1736.

William was 21 years old when The Seven Years War began in 1754.

He was 25 years old when he married Suzannah on December 27, 1757 in Barking, England. He was a tailor.

William was 77 years old when his son, Jermyn, passed away in 1810.

He was 79 years old when his wife passed away in 1812.

William was 80 years old when he passed away on January 25, 1813. A church was built over his grave.

THOMAS PATTISON[17]

Thomas was buried on March 27, 1804.
A church was built over his grave.

FRANK PEMBER[18]

Frank passed away in 1826.
A church was built over his grave.

MARTHA PEMBER[19]

Martha passed away in 1824.
A church was built over her grave.

PHILIP PEMBER[20]

Philip was buried on August 21, 1808.
A church was built over his grave.

PHILIP PEMBER[21]

Philip passed away in 1818.

A church was built over his grave.

SARAH PEMBER[22]

Sarah was buried on August 8, 1802.
A church was built over her grave.

THOMAS PEMBER[23]

Thomas passed away in 1820.

A church was built over his grave.

UNKNOWN PERKINS[24]

They were just a child when they were buried on April 20, 1796. A church was built over their grave.

JOHN PERKINS[25]

John was buried on February 18, 1799.
A church was built over his grave.

WILLIAM PERKINS[26]

William was buried on November 15, 1801. A church was built over his grave.

WILLIAM PERKINS[27]

William passed away in 1825.
A church was built over his grave.

BEMSLE PETERS[28]

Bemsle was born in Hebron, Connecticut on November 1, 1743

He was 10 years old when his father passed away in 1753. His brother, John, passed away in 1754.

Bemsle was 11 years old when his brother, Andrew, passed away in 1754.

He was 16 years old when his brother, William, passed away in 1760.

Bemsle was 17 years old when his brother, Joseph, passed away in 1761.

He was 18 years old when he married Annis on May 24, 1762 in Hebron, Connecticut.

Bemsle was 28 years old when his sister, Phebe, passed away in 1772.

He was 33 years old when his son, Bemsle, passed away in 1775.

Bemsle was 35 years old when his brother, Jonathan, passed away in 1778.

He was 40 years old when his mother passed away in 1784.

Bemsle was 54 years old when he was buried on October 4, 1798. A church was built over his grave.

THOMAS OLIPHANT PETRIE[29]

Thomas was born in April 1815 in Kingston, Frontenac, Upper Canada, British Colonial America.

He was a year old when he passed away on September 8, 1816. A church was built over his grave.

JOHN PHILIPS[30]

John was buried on July 5, 1795.

A church was built over his grave.

THOMAS PHILIPS[31]

Thomas was buried on November 26, 1805. A church was built over his grave.

THOMAS PHILIPS[32]

Thomas was a veteran when he was buried on January 1, 1810. A church was built over his grave.

JOSEPH PINKNEY[33]

Joseph was buried on October 7, 1805. A church was built over his grave.

THOMAS PLUMMER[34]

Thomas was buried on February 17, 1805.
A church was built over his grave.

JOHN PONETT[35]

John passed away in 1813.

A church was built over his grave.

JOHN POSEN[36]

John passed away in 1811.

A church was built over his grave.

THOMAS WILLIAM[37]

Thomas was born on October 25, 1784.

He was six years old when the first parliament of Upper Canada assembled on September 17, 1791.

Thomas was 19 years old when he passed away on June 16, 1804. A church was built over his grave.

WILLIAM PRAYLEY[38]

William passed away in 1812.
A church was built over his grave.

JOHN PRICE[39]

John passed away in 1813.

A church was built over his grave.

THOMAS PRICE[40]

Thomas was buried on May 9, 1809.

A church was built over his grave.

JOSEPH PRITCHARD[41]

Joseph was buried on August 10, 1802.
A church was built over his grave.

UNKNOWN PUREBECKS[42]

They were only a child when they were buried on August 4, 1792. A church was built over their grave.

EULIAL PURKIS[43]

Eulial passed away in 1824.

A church was built over his grave.

MARY RAINDLE[44]

Mary passed away in 1844.

A church was built over her grave.

WILLIAM RANDALL[45]

William passed away in 1819.
A church was built over his grave.

ANN RANKINS[46]

Ann was buried on September 30, 1795.
A church was built over her grave.

JOHN RASKHIP[47]

John passed away in 1813.

A church was built over his grave.

JANE REED[48]

Jane passed away in 1812.

A church was built over her grave.

UNKNOWN RENNY[49]

They were only a child when they were buried on March 20, 1797. A church was built over their grave.

PATRICK RICE[50]

Patrick served in the 60th regiment before he was buried on November 17, 1794,

A church was built over his grave.

JOHN DENNIS RICHARDSON[51]

John was born on January 7, 1817 in Kingston, Frontenac, Upper Canada, British Colonial America.

He passed away 23 days later on January 30th. A church was built over his grave which is located beneath the parish hall.

SARAH (ASHMORE) RICHARDSON[52]

Sarah was born in Kings Norton, England in 1751.

She was 19 years old when the Boston Tea Party took place in 1770.

Sarah was 24 years old when the "Shot Heard Around The World" took place on April 18, 1775.

She was 58 years old when she was buried on May 13, 1809. Sarah is buried with her grandson, John Dennis Richardson, beneath the parish hall.

THOMAS RICHARDSON[53]

Thomas was buried on October 11, 1804.
A church was built over his grave.

JOHN RIDLEY[54]

John was buried on July 14, 1804.

A church was built over his grave.

WILLIAM RIPP[55]

William was buried on August 16, 1795.
A church was built over his grave.

JAMES ROBBINS[56]

James passed away in 1825.

A church was built over his grave.

JOSEPH ROBBINS[57]

Joseph passed away in 1819.

A church was built over his grave.

JOHN ROBINS[58]

John was buried on November 20, 1794. A church was built over his grave.

MARGARET ROBINS[59]

Margaret was buried on December 28, 1803. A church was built over her grave.

MRS. UNKNOWN ROBINSON[60]

She was buried on October 17, 1802.

A church was built over her grave.

BETSY ROBINSON[61]

Betsy was buried on September 29, 1794.
A church was built over her grave.

JAMES ROBINSON[62]

James passed away in 1819.

A church was built over his grave.

MARY ROBINSON[63]

Mary Robinson passed away in 1816.

A church was built over her grave.

CPT. THOMAS ROBISON[64]

Thomas was buried on March 29, 1806.
A church was built over his grave.

WILLIAM ROBISON[65]

William was born in Portland, Maine in 1789.

He was 62 years old when he was buried on March 12, 1851.

BENJAMIN ROCHELEAU[66]

Benjamin was buried on May 2, 1803.
A church was built over his grave.

JOSEPH R. ROCK[67]

Joseph was buried on June 2, 1806,
A church was built over his grave.

ELIZA ROGERS[68]

Eliza was buried on August 8, 1806.

A church was built over her grave.

JAMES ROGGIE[69]

James was buried on May 16, 1806.

A church was built over his grave.

JANE ROGGIE[70]

Jane was buried on May 14, 1806.

A church was built over her grave.

UNKNOWN RUSSELL[71]

They were only a child when they were buried on March 8, 1793. A church was built over their grave.

ABIGAIL RUSSELL[72]

Abigail was buried on October 12, 1791. A church was built over her grave.

LUCY RUSSELL[73]

Lucy was buried on March 11, 1806.

A church was built over her grave.

MARY RUSSELL[74]

Mary passed away in 1815.

A church was built over her grave.

---

[1] https://www.wikitree.com/genealogy/O'Reiley-Family-Tree-6

[2] https://www.wikitree.com/genealogy/Oliver-Family-Tree-15934

[3] https://www.wikitree.com/genealogy/Oliver-Family-Tree-15935

[4] https://www.wikitree.com/genealogy/Oliver-Family-Tree-15936

[5] https://www.wikitree.com/genealogy/Olkot-Family-Tree-1

[6] https://www.wikitree.com/genealogy/Olson-Family-Tree-8654

[7] https://www.wikitree.com/genealogy/Owen-Family-Tree-12892

[8] https://www.wikitree.com/genealogy/Page-Family-Tree-15921

[9] https://www.wikitree.com/genealogy/Paine-Family-Tree-4462

[10] https://www.wikitree.com/genealogy/Parker-Family-Tree-48088

[11] https://www.wikitree.com/genealogy/Parker-Family-Tree-48089

[12] https://www.wikitree.com/genealogy/Patrick-Family-Tree-6561

[13] https://www.wikitree.com/genealogy/Patrick-Family-Tree-6562

[14] https://www.wikitree.com/genealogy/Aldham-Family-Tree-57

[15] https://www.wikitree.com/genealogy/Bull-Family-Tree-5651

[16] https://www.wikitree.com/genealogy/Patrick-Family-Tree-6563

[17] https://www.wikitree.com/genealogy/Pattison-Family-Tree-1659

[18] https://www.wikitree.com/genealogy/Pember-Family-Tree-207

[19] https://www.wikitree.com/genealogy/Pember-Family-Tree-208

[20] https://www.wikitree.com/genealogy/Pember-Family-Tree-209

[21] https://www.wikitree.com/genealogy/Pember-Family-Tree-210

[22] https://www.wikitree.com/genealogy/Pember-Family-Tree-211

[23] https://www.wikitree.com/genealogy/Pember-Family-Tree-212

[24] https://www.wikitree.com/genealogy/Perkins-Family-Tree-19715

[25] https://www.wikitree.com/genealogy/Perkins-Family-Tree-19716

[26] https://www.wikitree.com/genealogy/Perkins-Family-Tree-19717

[27] https://www.findagrave.com/memorial/175056163/william-perkins

[28] https://www.wikitree.com/genealogy/Peters-Family-Tree-16328

[29] https://www.wikitree.com/genealogy/Petrie-Family-Tree-2097

[30] https://www.findagrave.com/memorial/173932740/john-philips

[31] https://www.wikitree.com/genealogy/Philips-Family-Tree-2132

[32] https://www.wikitree.com/genealogy/Philips-Family-Tree-2133

[33] https://www.wikitree.com/genealogy/Pinkney-Family-Tree-487

[34] https://www.wikitree.com/genealogy/Plummer-Family-Tree-4466

[35] https://www.wikitree.com/genealogy/Ponett-Family-Tree-1

[36] https://www.findagrave.com/memorial/175056354/john-posen

[37] https://www.wikitree.com/genealogy/Powell-Family-Tree-24029

[38] https://www.wikitree.com/genealogy/Prayley-Family-Tree-1

[39] https://www.wikitree.com/genealogy/Price-Family-Tree-28830

[40] https://www.wikitree.com/genealogy/Price-Family-Tree-28831

[41] https://www.wikitree.com/genealogy/Pritchard-Family-Tree-3125

[42] https://www.wikitree.com/genealogy/Purebecks-Family-Tree-1

[43] https://www.wikitree.com/genealogy/Purkis-Family-Tree-138

[44] https://www.wikitree.com/genealogy/Raindle-Family-Tree-7

[45] https://www.wikitree.com/genealogy/Randall-Family-Tree-10439

[46] https://www.wikitree.com/genealogy/Rankins-Family-Tree-175

[47] https://www.wikitree.com/genealogy/Raskhip-Family-Tree-1

[48] https://www.wikitree.com/genealogy/Reed-Family-Tree-30681

[49] https://www.wikitree.com/genealogy/Renny-Family-Tree-99

[50] https://www.wikitree.com/genealogy/Rice-Family-Tree-20862

[51] https://www.wikitree.com/genealogy/Richardson-Family-Tree-32956

[52] https://www.wikitree.com/genealogy/Ashmore-Family-Tree-1115
[53] https://www.wikitree.com/genealogy/Richardson-Family-Tree-34202
[54] https://www.wikitree.com/genealogy/Ridley-Family-Tree-2462
[55] https://www.wikitree.com/genealogy/Ripp-Family-Tree-125
[56] https://www.wikitree.com/genealogy/Robbins-Family-Tree-10513
[57] https://www.wikitree.com/genealogy/Robbins-Family-Tree-10514
[58] https://www.wikitree.com/genealogy/Robins-Family-Tree-2809
[59] https://www.wikitree.com/genealogy/Robins-Family-Tree-2810
[60] https://www.wikitree.com/genealogy/Unknown-Family-Tree-618522
[61] https://www.wikitree.com/genealogy/Robinson-Family-Tree-53878
[62] https://www.wikitree.com/genealogy/Robinson-Family-Tree-53879
[63] https://www.wikitree.com/genealogy/Unknown-Family-Tree-618525
[64] https://www.wikitree.com/genealogy/Robison-Family-Tree-2630
[65] https://www.wikitree.com/genealogy/Robison-Family-Tree-2433
[66] https://www.wikitree.com/genealogy/Rocheleau-Family-Tree-432
[67] https://www.wikitree.com/genealogy/Rock-Family-Tree-1732
[68] https://www.wikitree.com/genealogy/Rogers-Family-Tree-40152
[69] https://www.wikitree.com/genealogy/Roggie-Family-Tree-16
[70] https://www.wikitree.com/genealogy/Roggie-Family-Tree-17
[71] https://www.wikitree.com/genealogy/Russell-Family-Tree-32463
[72] https://www.wikitree.com/genealogy/Russell-Family-Tree-32464
[73] https://www.wikitree.com/genealogy/Russell-Family-Tree-32465
[74] https://www.wikitree.com/genealogy/Russell-Family-Tree-32466

Don't miss out!

Visit the website below and you can sign up to receive emails whenever Angeline Gallant publishes a new book. There's no charge and no obligation.

https://books2read.com/r/B-A-QGSI-OAEBC

BOOKS 2 READ

Connecting independent readers to independent writers.

Also by Angeline Gallant

A Dragon's Diary

Dreaming of Dragons

Blood and Spirit Saga

The Rising Wind

Calling Her Heart

Whisper of the Heart

Calling Her Heart Volumes 1 & 2: A Small Town Romance Collection

No Turning Back

Calling Her Heart volumes 3 & 4

Forsake Me Not

Hear My Cry

FORGET ME NOT

Victoria, Ontario's Babies 1894 - 1895

Guardian of the Heart
Fallen Petals

Keeper Of Secrets
A Lady's Secret

Kingston's Love Chronicles
Springtime Promises

Midnight's Awakening
Heart of the Storm
Walking Through The Storm
Walking Through The Storm
Fighting the Storm
Call Me Cursed
Heart of the Storm

Secrets of the Underworld
Deklan's Dragons

Tell My Story Collection
Tell My Story: Germany 1851
Tell My Story: England 1852

Whispers From The Garrison Church

The Dervock Legacy
Echoes of Dervock

The Grave Whisperer
German Prisoners of War in Canada
Cataraqui United Church Cemetery
Whispers of Kingston
Wedding Bells in Kingston, Ontario, Canada 1923
St. Paul's Anglican Churchyard A-B
St. Paul's Anglican Churchyard C-D
St. Paul's Anglican Churchyard E - F
St. Paul's Anglican Churchyard, Kingston, Ontario, Canada G - H
St. Paul's Anglican Churchyard J - N
St. Paul's Anglican Churchyard O - R
St. Paul's Anglican Churchyard, Kingston, Ontario, Canada S - T
St. Paul's Anglican Churchyard, Kingston, Ontario T - Z
Small Graveyards & Burial Grounds: Kingston, Ontario, Canada
Cataraqui United Church Cemetery 1
Cataraqui United Church Cemetery 2
Cataraqui United Church Cemetary 3
Cataraqui United Church Cemetery 4
Cataraqui United Church Cemetery 5
Beth Israel Cemetery
Cataraqui United Church Cemetery 6
Beneath the Surface: Echoes from Beth Israel Cemetery
Grave Tales: Discovering the Lives of Beth Israel
Whispers Beneath St. Paul's

The Timeless Veil

Eternal Devotion

The Wolf Whisperer Series

Captured Heart

Fate's Legacy

Mohawk Valley

Cry of a Warrior

Wolf Whisperer volumes 1 & 2

Endless White

The Wolf Whisperer volumes 1 & 2

Timeless

The Time Keeper's Sanctuary

Timeless Whispers of Dervock Saga

Secrets of Dervock

Standalone

Winds of Change vol 1-3

Watch for more at https://www.goodreads.com/author/show/19703964.Angeline_Gallant.

About the Author

Angeline Gallant traces her roots through generations of Old Stock Canadian heritage, her passion for genealogy as deep and enduring as the forests and fields her ancestors once walked. With a reverence for history and an eye for detail, she weaves stories from the fragments of lives left behind in letters, records, and weathered headstones.

An avid reader and devoted writer, Angeline brings the past to life with a curiosity for heraldry and a deep love for the landscapes that shaped her family's story. Each name and date she uncovers feels less like history and more like coming home, a familiar echo in the vast tapestry of time. For her, these stories are not forgotten—they live, breathing in the quiet spaces of memory and tradition, a testament to lives once lived, now eternal in the pages of her books.

Read more at https://www.goodreads.com/author/show/19703964.Angeline_Gallant.

www.ingramcontent.com/pod-product-compliance
Ingram Content Group UK Ltd.
Pitfield, Milton Keynes, MK11 3LW, UK
UKHW021656190726
13853UKWH00001B/286

9 798215 663462